Praise for Own Your Worth

In *Own Your Worth*, Lesley Wirth gently encourages her readers to view struggles with eating and negative body image as an invitation to embark on a spiritual journey, through which they can discover the beauty of who they really are. Using tales from her own recovery from disordered eating, self-loathing, and body hatred to illuminate the way step-by-step, she shows how self-acceptance and self-compassion can create a pathway towards freedom.

~ Anita Johnston. Ph.D. Author, *Eating in the Light of the Moon*
and Creator of Light of the Moon Café
LightoftheMoonCafe.com

- Clinical Director & Founder of 'Ai Pono Maui Residential Eating Disorders Facility
- Clinical Director & Founder of the 'Ai Pono Intensive Out-Patient Eating Disorders Programs
- Director & Co-founder of Anorexia & Bulimia Center of Hawaii; Clinical Advisor to Focus Treatment Center for Eating Disorders

When reading this book, one can feel Lesley's love for those who struggle with food issues and self esteem challenges as well as her passion to share her hard-won learnings with others. This book is a both blessing and a must-read for women who are searching for a new way to view themselves and their world.

~ Trisha Kelly, Co-Founder of The Soul Institute
and Soul of Yoga
SoulofYoga.com

Own Your Worth takes you right to the core of what perpetuates disordered eating and a negative image of your body. It provides you a pathway out of the madness and back into your heart. Thank you, Lesley, for your vulnerability and truth.

~ Lilia Birem, Teacher of Energetics and Holistic Life Coach
LiliaBirem.com

Own Your Worth takes you from victim to victor, fearful to empowered, and self-critical to self-compassionate. In essence, this book provides a roadmap to a more heart-centered life and the freedom that comes with it.

~ Deborah Brenner-Liss, Ph.D., Director of the Association of Professionals Treating Eating Disorders
AptedSF.org

I can confidently say that Lesley's last name was of Divine orchestration. *Own Your Worth* takes you from unworthiness to knowing your Worth. Read it once, then read it again!

~ Dayna Dunbar, Award-Winning Visionary Novelist
DaynaDunbar.com

This book sheds new light on how we perpetuate our suffering with food… and offers hope for a new way. Written by one who has been there and found the answers that work, this book is a must-read!

~ Martha Vachon, Lifecoach
LifeCoachMartha.com

Own Your Worth

A Spiritual Journey through Food Compulsion to Self-Love

Copyright

Published by Soul Light Publishing
Own Your Worth
A Spiritual Journey through Food Compulsion to Self-love
Copyright © 2014 by Lesley Wirth

It is my intention to support all women desiring to break free of shame and judgment and begin to embody Love and compassion. Therefore, if you wish to use the contents of this book to support others, simply email me per my copyright policy, as all rights are reserved. No part of this book may be used without written consent, so let's connect and get you started on learning how to best apply *Own Your Worth* to your program as an adjunct support. Collaboration is something I am honored to be a part of, and I look forward to sharing with you the program that came from this book! For permissions or information on bulk purchases, educational use or book excerpts, please send an email to lesley@lesleywirth.com.

This book is not intended as a substitute for treatment of psychological or emotional conditions that may require evaluation and care from a physician or appropriate mental health professional. The intent of the author is that the book be a source of inspiration and support for one's quest for physical, mental, and spiritual wellbeing.

ISBN: 978-0-9862966-0-4

Own Your Worth

A Spiritual Journey through Food Compulsion to Self-Love

Lesley Wirth

Dedication

To all of you who have forgotten your worth and value while on your journey . . . May you find freedom from suffering and reconnect to the Light within you.

Contents

Acknowledgments	xiii
Introduction	1
Chapter 1: The Million Dollar Question	7
Chapter 2: Belief Systems and Paradigms	15
Chapter 3: Rewriting Your Story	27
Chapter 4: The Rules	33
Chapter 5: From Powerless to Finding Strength in the Divine Mother	39
Chapter 6: Healing through Creative Expression	49
Chapter 7: Setting an Intention	57
Chapter 8: Hope	63
Chapter 9: Creating Your Destiny	69
Chapter 10: Honesty and the Beauty of Vulnerability	75
Chapter 11: Your Soul's Compass	79
Chapter 12: Celebration	83
Continuing the Journey	89
About the Author	91
Notes	93

Acknowledgments

It is with Divine support and Grace that I have written this book. I bow to this energy first and foremost, and am in deep gratitude for the support I received on many levels. With gratitude and thanks to my editor Deborah Louise Brown; to my Earth Angel Lilia Birem for teaching me through example how to be an empowered, awake woman; and to Drs. Ron and Mary Helnick for teaching me the principles and tools of spiritual psychology.

Introduction

You may have experienced a life challenge that left you reeling. You may have spent days or years feeling unworthy or like you're not enough. And maybe those feelings have caused you pain and shame because you couldn't seem to shake them and move on.

I know all too well about pain and shame and not being able to shake some very debilitating and serious patterns. I understand self-hatred and compulsion expressed through my thirteen-year journey through severe anorexia, bulimia, compulsive eating, and exercise addiction. After years of healing work and completing my Master's in Spiritual

Psychology, I felt called to write a book designed to help women find their value, worth, and experience self-love. *Own Your Worth: A Spiritual Journey Through Food Compulsion to Self-Love* is about my journey, yes, but more importantly, it is a guidebook that will help you find personal value, worth and love inside yourself. You will learn how to use your soul's wisdom to rise above old patterns and unleash a beautiful life.

Whatever shape your struggle takes, understand one thing: *improving yourself* is not the answer. Fulfillment, joy and "dreams come true" are accomplished when you come into resonance with your true nature, *your soul*.

I am sharing my story and the guiding principles that helped me transform my life, in hopes that you will be able to do the same. *Own Your Worth* is about hope and freedom. Everyone deserves to live a life of hope and freedom. Everyone.

The chapters are comprised of personal stories and activities. These activities are designed to assist you in working through your challenges as well as help you cultivate a sense of self-love, empowerment, and a deeper connection to your inner guidance system.

You will learn new ways of relating to yourself, your life, and your relationship with food.

The activities found within this guidebook are tools you can use long after you complete it. It is my hope that the activities support you in taking greater dominion over your life as you continually implement the lessons and skills you have cultivated. The amount of transformation you will experience is up to you. As with most anything, what you put in is what you get out. Personally I find this to be very exciting, because it leaves you in charge of your growth. *You hold the key to your own liberation.*

My Message to You

There are six words that I want you to hear, know, and believe about yourself – and those six words are, *there is nothing wrong with you.* You are not your behavior with food. You are not the thoughts in your head. You are not your emotions. You are not even the sum total of all these parts. You are so much more. You, my sweet one, are a Spiritual Being having a human experience.

And as a Spiritual Being having a human experience, you are here dealing with some pretty intense human stuff at times! Living with a painful relationship with food is not easy. But, if you are willing, it can actually serve you. You can use it as a stepping stone to self-love and self-compassion. You can use it to come home to yourself, and build a beautiful relationship with the most important person in your life: You.

If you are in recovery, or have been for years, you may have found using a spiritual approach to be helpful in your process. It allows us to give depth and meaning to something beyond our personality self; our ego, which is where any sort of addictive tendency resides. By choosing to view addictive tendencies as serving a higher purpose, we live a life that is happening *for* us, rather than to us. We then have the opportunity to use our challenges as a doorway to something much greater than simply releasing symptoms. As good as symptom free sounds, the peace, freedom, and joy that we all crave, does not come automatically from changing our patterns. Trust me on this one. I have not only lived it personally, but have also worked with many women who are still miserable after they change their behavior. It wasn't until they started to change the relationship they had with themselves that they were able to connect to peace.

Because an eating disorder, food challenges, or an addiction of any kind, is something that we are using to cope, it can be put into the category of our human experience. Our human self, or personality self, is what is trying to cope. Our spiritual self is doing just fine. In all situations and under all circumstances, our soul is steadfast and sure. It is safe and it is Light. It is our anchor and a place we can start to connect to inside of us to help us alleviate our suffering.

As a Spiritual Being we are here to go through experiences that will give us the opportunity to connect more deeply with our Inherent Nature, which is love. This is the ultimate curriculum for all of us. No matter what we are learning in this life, all paths are trying to lead us back to love. This may seem esoteric and unimportant to you at this point, but as you read the contents of this book, you will gain an understanding as to why this is the ultimate opportunity for happiness and bliss. Our addictive tendencies can turn out to be the biggest blessings of our lives.

I have learned a lot in my twenty-year journey with food and my body. What I can confidentially share with you, is that the growth that comes from staying connected to my spiritual journey has allowed me more freedom than any other person, plan, or program. My job is to learn how to love myself no matter what I am thinking, feeling, doing, or experiencing. This is the ultimate path of a warrior. And although counter-intuitive to many who are trying to "fix" themselves, this way of being is what affords the greatest transformation.

Chapter 1
The Million Dollar Question

*Out beyond ideas of wrongdoing and rightdoing,
there is a field. I will meet you there.*

~ Rumi

I stood there, looking in the mirror at the woman I never accepted and stared into her eyes. I felt no connection. No love. All I saw was resolve to make myself "better." I looked at the face staring back at me and I yearned for it to be different. And then I felt ashamed that I was caught up in my looks. So, I stood there, in my self-rejection and my shame, as I fantasized about being someone else. Someone who looked different. Someone who actually liked herself.

I turned to look at my profile and shuddered at my lack of jaw line. I thought about my crooked nose and my muscular legs. I was so uncomfortable in my skin I did not know what to do with myself except to try and work harder at becoming thinner and prettier. And so it went for over half of my life. Until one day, the fear of living in self-loathing forever caused my soul to cry out for me to wake up. It screamed at me. It pleaded with me to live a heart-centered and full life. It whispered that peace was possible and that I, too, could experience joy.

I was clear on where I wanted to go – freedom – but I had no idea how to get there. I knew I needed help. I had already been hospitalized for anorexia twice and at this point was in my eleventh year of bulimia. Not knowing what else to do, I immersed myself in a twelve-step program for overeaters. I got a sponsor and worked the steps. It changed my life. And here is why: I wanted it to! I was willing to do whatever it took for me to create a new life for myself. I participated in meetings, cultivated deep friendships and sponsored others. It was the first time I had ever felt a part of something that accepted all of me. I started to come out of hiding. It helped me reopen my heart.

I learned how to become accountable for my behaviors, my choices, and my own life. And I became more comfortable looking at and talking about my inner world of thoughts and feelings. Yet I was still very caught up in needing to be seen in a positive light. I needed others to think I had it all together and figured out. I only shared so much. I shared my inner experience only to the point that I felt they would not reject or judge me. I was afraid if they knew the parts of me that I still wanted to hide, they would not want me. It is true that I found a new level of authenticity in program, but I still found myself hiding a bit. I still felt I needed to prove my value and worth and tried to present a positive image while in recovery. I was afraid I would lose credibility and that my recovery needed to look just so. I was trying to get my sense of self-worth through this new, "better" version of myself, my recovered self. And now that I look back on it, it was exhausting!

Prior to program, the way I had experienced a sense of self-worth and value in the world was through my body's appearance. And when I no longer was focused on becoming thinner, I channeled that same need into validation through the image I tried to maintain. I thought if I kept talking about how much freedom I had, how much my life had changed, and how things were finally "perfect," I would be deemed worthy by others. I thought this way I would be wanted and would receive love, and thus be able to accept myself. Rather than asking if I was good enough, I could have been asking more liberating questions. Do I accept myself? Can I be okay with the places inside that I am proud of as well as the places inside I've judged? And the million dollar question…"Do I own my self-worth?" This question is such a big one, and to be honest, most of us do not. We look for validation, acceptance, and love outside of ourselves. This is not earth-shattering news. You know this. I know this. It is a world-wide epidemic, this sense of unworthiness. It seems to just be a part of the human condition. It doesn't make us *weak*, or *bad*, or *not enough* to have this experience. It is common and it is painful. So let's use this pain of living our lives seeking acceptance to cover our sense of inadequacy to motivate us to find our worth inside of ourselves.

If you can let yourself off the hook and accept that you are a human being who sometimes feels okay about herself, and others times is desperate for a sense of acceptance, then you create space in your world. And within that space, you are allowed to be all of yourself and start to make peace with those places you keep trying to change. It doesn't matter if it's a behavior, a thought, or a feeling; if you are making it wrong, you will suffer. You are allowed to be and feel whatever is authentic for you in that given moment. In other words, you get to stop wasting your energy trying to be something else. What if you could just let it be okay that you feel what you do?

What if it could be okay that sometimes you experience feelings of unworthiness? That does not make you weak or less than. It makes you a human being. Your feelings actually have absolutely no bearing on your worth. Your worth is inherent. It exists despite what is going on for you.

Our worth comes from our Essence. Our True Self. We are all infinitely worthy because we are the Divine in flesh; it is within us. Not one person on the entire planet is an exception to this truth. Not one. And because of this, no matter what we think, feel, or do, we all are equally worthy. Our mind will come up with ways to keep us locked into the misunderstanding that we have to somehow prove or earn our worth. Call it out. Don't fall for it. It simply isn't true.

The truth is we are infinitely worthy simply because we exist. We are an extension of the supreme truth, which is love. This is our True Nature, and it is time we come together in this declaration. It is up to us to awaken one another to the radiant truth within each other. But first we must awaken to this truth within ourselves. We can only illuminate in one another what is already illuminated within ourselves.

By recovering our sense of self-worth, we empower ourselves to simply be. We are allowed to have our full range of human emotions and experiences. We are allowed to be all of ourselves. If you knew that you could be all of you, and continue to be loved, how would your life change? What could you start to look at and explore, rather than run away from? How would your perception of yourself change?

What would it be like to be able to start to recognize that everything, "good" and "bad," was just our ego? What would it be like to live understanding that there really is a place beyond duality? Rumi's quote is a representation of this. He says, "Out beyond ideas of wrongdoing and rightdoing, there is a field. I will meet you there." He is speaking of the place that exists beyond duality, beyond our ego's measurement stick. Rumi is speaking of our Divine Nature, which cannot be compromised. No matter what. It just is.

Activity: Another Divine Being Having a Human Experience

Grab a pen and your journal and sit someplace where you will be uninterrupted. Take a few moments to settle into your body and become fully present. Relax. Breathe. Then answer the following questions:

- How would your life be different if you knew you were lovable no matter what you were thinking, feeling, or doing? Specifically how would your inner experience be different?

- What parts of yourself do you hide out of fear of what it would mean about you if you allowed them to exist?

- How is this impacting your life?

- What is one step you can take toward being more transparent with your humanness?

Chapter 2
Belief Systems and Paradigms

If you find yourself believing that you must always be the way you have always been, you are arguing against growth.

~Wayne Dyer

Believing my worth and value depended on the way I looked and how others reacted to me was something I was so wrapped up in, I didn't even know it was my reality. I had no idea that I was viewing myself and the world through such a distorted lens... one that seemed to filter everything through the lens of *I am not enough*. Being it was the only lens I had ever seen through, I didn't know any different. Being that it was the only paradigm I had ever known, I thought what I was seeing was the truth.

This paradigm resulted in my trying to find a way to feel I was enough and prove I was enough. I tried through my physical appearance and through trying to win others' approval. This "I am not enough" world I was living in was not created overnight. In fact, it was developed at a very young age and reinforced as the years went by. I did not question it until I discovered that I could decide for myself what I believed to be true.

The real truth, that I was enough, am enough, and always will be enough, was something I had to discover on my own. And I did this by opening to the idea that something else could be true. I made a conscious effort to heal whatever it was that had me buying into this distorted view of myself. I knew that my Essence was pure, worthy, and infinitely good, so if I kept getting caught up believing otherwise, it was up to me to discover, heal, and discard the lies I was carrying. I had to heal my belief system, my paradigm.

So what exactly is a paradigm? Simply put, a paradigm is our personal reality; it is life as we know it. And life as we know it today is made up of many years of experiences and the conclusions we drew about them. When we look out into the world, we see things through a habitual eye, a personal lens. This habitual eye influences how we see ourselves as well. So if we do not like what we see when we look at ourselves, we need to look at the lens we are peering through. We have to ask ourselves, *What is going on that has me seeing things the way I do?*

Our personal lens is largely shaped by our unconscious mind. This part of our brain is formed during childhood and influences us every single day. Because the unconscious mind is such a massive part of our life experience it is important to explore what has been stored there, outside of our conscious awareness. If we want to transform our patterns, heal our suffering, and reshape our paradigm, exploring the lens we see through is vital. We can get so sidetracked by what is happening in the present, that we do not realize that what we are *experiencing now* has been shaped by the past. We must stop and question objectively if what we think, feel, and believe is the ultimate truth or if it is something we have been carrying with us for years, or even lifetimes. To be clear, I do not believe in dwelling in the past, but I do believe it has its place in our journey to liberation. Looking into our history can provide information we can use to create the lives we want for ourselves in the here and now.

By getting to the core of the issue, the place where the paradigm developed in the first place, a person gets a clear picture of what happened that caused the paradigm and has the opportunity to heal it. It is like pulling a vegetable out of the soil – you want to go all the way to the root. Think of what you get when you pull the entire vegetable out, root and all, versus when you pull just from the surface level. When you pull from the root, you remove the whole thing. When you pull from the ground level, you only get a part of it, the top of it.

So, if we just focus on what is happening in the here and now, we will transform only so much, leaving the roots in fertile soil, ready to sprout all over again. The key is to get to the root of our belief systems and perceptions. When we can go back in time to when the issue first developed, we are able to heal things at the level that is needed for lasting transformation. *We can heal at the root level.*

When it comes to how we eat, the same rule holds true. If we only look at the surface issue (the way we eat) we never get to the core of the problem. And if we want true freedom and a life that we feel really good about, then tending to the surface is not enough. Oftentimes, our issue is not what it appears to be. It is not about the food, the money, or the co-dependent relationships we have. The issue is really about what is inside of us that we are trying to work out but don't know how. We act it out through food, relationships, and so forth. Food and body image are simply areas where unresolved material tries to resolve itself. The real issue is rooted much deeper within us, and when we can get to that core place, we can dramatically transform our lives.

So, for compulsive overeaters, or anyone with food issues, simply managing food is going to create a temporary fix. How many times have you changed your behaviors just to find yourself right back where you started? This is not because you failed, or that you can't do it. What it is, however, is a clear representation that your inner garden needs a little tending. And maybe even a little sunshine.

Activity: Our Lens

Our belief system runs much deeper than we may be aware of. In fact, we oftentimes hold beliefs in our unconscious mind that are the opposite of what our conscious mind considers to be the truth. For example, have you ever found yourself in a circumstance in which you were upset about something that you didn't feel warranted such an intense reaction? Many people label this "over-reacting." But to some place inside of you, the reaction was warranted. Some belief within you was activated.

Discovering the belief systems that are operating underneath our thoughts, emotions, and actions brings forth a wonderful opportunity for healing and inner freedom. And in replacing these ill-serving belief systems with new beliefs, we have the chance to create a future that is more in alignment, not with our old programming, but with what we really want.

Given our belief systems are frequently unconscious, it can be very challenging to access them on our own. This activity is designed to get you moving in the right direction, toward the root of the issue. You can use it for any issue that arises in your life, as it is a tool for you to use when you are having a hard time.

Inside our unconscious mind (where our beliefs are) there are all sorts of old perceptions of ourselves. These old perceptions are what we want to access, and we can do so by personifying them as our younger self. I first experienced the benefits of personifying through my work with one of my spiritual mentors and friends, Lilia Birem. And during my graduate studies at the University of Santa Monica, I learned how to get in touch with my inner child. The blending of these ideas has been extremely helpful for me in my journey, and now I would like to share them with you. We start by allowing past memories to come forward from the perspective of our younger self, so as to attune to the beliefs that were anchored in at that time. You see, it is these beliefs that are creating the issues today.

Part 1: Your Younger Self

Before you begin this exercise, decide upon a place you can complete it without being interrupted. If you can, place yourself somewhere comfortable and inviting to you. This helps you open up and relax. Take several minutes and be mindful of your body, sensing the breath move in and out as your chest rises and falls. *Feel* the breath. Once you feel you have centered yourself, you are ready to begin.

1. Think back to when you were a little child. Now think of a time that was very challenging for you. Maybe you were frustrated, deeply hurt, or scared. Name this time out loud by titling it. For example, *the time my neighbor told me I was worthless.*

2. Imagine watching this younger version of you as though you were watching a movie. See her as vividly as you can. Notice what she looks like, what she is doing, and what is

happening around her as you imagine this challenging time. Remaining mindful that you are separate from her, and that you are simply watching, start to describe out loud what you see.

3. Now start to name what is happening inside of her. Is she going blank? Is she shutting down, doubting herself, blaming herself, angry but too afraid to show it? Whatever her inner experience is, see if you can *sense* what it is. Trust what you sense instead of trying to think about what you imagine she "should" be feeling. Then, speak out loud what is happening inside of her.

4. Becoming a little more intimate, see if you can sense what she is making this all mean about her. For example, *if she is shutting down and is deeply hurt in response to her neighbor telling her she is worthless, what does she believe about herself? She may believe he is right and that she is worthless and has no value. Or she may conclude that there must be something inherently wrong with her.* Whatever it is, if you bring your attention from your head to your body, the most appropriate answer will be there. You do this by sitting quietly and not trying to come up with an

answer. Let it come to you through sitting in silence and being present. Name out loud what she made this mean about her.

5. Now allow *her* to complete the following sentence:

   When I was experiencing this challenging time in my life, I made it mean _____ about me.

6. Take a moment and really let that sink in. Think about that sweet little one who actually believed something bad about herself based on something that happened when she was just a little, innocent girl. Imagine all that pain and suffering she must have felt, as you look at her through compassionate eyes.

Part 2: Compassionate Eyes

No matter how old we are our unconscious mind is with us, holding old perceptions and beliefs from our younger years. As adults, we have an opportunity to examine these old beliefs and relate to them in a completely new way. Rather than shutting ourselves down or trying to "fix" ourselves, we can look back in time and see where the original imprint was created and decide if it is accurate. Now we can hold compassion for our younger self's interpretation of reality, rather than believe we must be at fault and that we need to be "fixed." This allows us to stop our habitual responses, and create more loving and empowered choices for ourselves in thought and actions.

1. Now that you have seen the younger you through compassionate eyes, bring forward something in your life that is challenging for you right now, something that when you connect to it, you feel unpleasant emotions. Name this out loud.

2. Just like you did in Part 1, imagine yourself in this circumstance. *Consider how somewhere inside you still have that innocent little girl who has tender feelings and insecurities.* Imagine that she is the one going through this challenging time. Really try to connect to her by tuning into what she is feeling and believing about herself.

3. Place your hand on your heart. Ask yourself what you would tell her if she was going through what you are

experiencing today. Tell her your answer.

4. Grab a journal and a pen to record what you have learned, as well as any guidance you may have received.

5. Write the younger version of yourself a note, acknowledging her for all she has done for you.

Chapter 3
Rewriting Your Story

Tenderness and kindness are not signs of weakness and despair but manifestations of strength and resolution.

~ Kahlil Gibran

I have looked thoroughly at my own belief systems, and how they have shaped my life. I can confidently say I have done a significant rewrite. I have written a new story for myself. This new story is one of the many blessings that comes from the willingness to do transformational work. We all have the opportunity to become conscious authors of our lives. We do this by recognizing why we interpreted things the way we did in the past, and healing the place within us that still holds on to it as truth. We free ourselves of our limited understanding by updating our perceptions through deep compassion and awareness. We release, heal, and update our beliefs. No one can do this for us. It is up to each and every one of us to be responsible enough to become a loving author for ourselves and humanity.

One way in which I have rewritten my story involves how I feel about myself as an emotional being. I cannot count how many times I have heard, "People with eating disorders just don't know how to deal with their feelings." While this could be true, I find it to be an overly-simplified statement. There is so much more to our relationship to food than our emotional state. We have karma, biological predispositions, thoughts, and habitual response patterns, and the one thing that ties all of these together, our belief system. We can truly alter everything by shifting our belief systems.

Like many who have had an eating disorder, I was an extremely sensitive kid. I felt things to a great degree, and my body seemed to pick up on things that no one else was talking about. For me, this resulted in a sense of overwhelm. I was not sure how to navigate in a world of such intensity. And, not understanding it was a gift, I turned on myself for being so sensitive. I bought into the belief that I was somehow "too sensitive," and that this made me weak. I could not understand why I felt so easily derailed and like I was going to vomit if I saw someone hurting. The energy I felt of those around me seemed to take over my system, and pretty soon I felt victim to it. I didn't know how to use my sensitivity as an asset.

As an adult I have continued to experience this level of sensitivity, but have learned how my sensitive nature is actually a great gift from God that is available to me to use as a resource for navigating life. This shift in perspective has nothing to do with looking on the positive side, and everything to do with how I genuinely view my reality today. I now see how my sensitivity serves me with clarity, direction, and guidance. I understand it is an invaluable inner resource that guides me based on my intuitive knowing.

So how does one go about making these rewrites actually happen? How can we truly and authentically feel and believe something different? The process you just completed on your belief systems is the first step. You looked into how you were holding things (what you were making them mean) and did some brainstorming on ways in which you could hold things differently. You exercised a new muscle – a muscle of opening up to new ways of relating to yourself and the world. From here, we learn how to create a new definition of reality through looking at how things are *serving* us.

From the perspective that everything we possess is here

to serve us in some way, we can easily find the value in what we are experiencing. Rather than alienating ourselves for what our authentic experience is, we learn how to use it as a way to be more empowered in this lifetime. We learn how to make our authentic experience work for us, because I can guarantee you, that is ultimately what it is trying to do.

So, with that my friend, let the rewriting begin …

Activity: Rewriting Your Story

Pull out a journal and start to bullet point the things in your life that you find challenging. After you have made your list of the most challenging areas, go back and briefly write why it is challenging for you.

For example:

- <u>I am too sensitive</u>: I am afraid I can't handle certain situations. I find that I am actually keeping myself from doing the things I want to do because of it.

- <u>I hate my body</u>: I wake up every morning in despair over the way I look when I see myself in the mirror. I am too embarrassed to wear shorts or a cute little dress. Sometimes I just want to crawl out of my skin!

And so on…

Now that you have described the story your mind tells you, start to explore the possibility that within each of the bullet points listed, there are opportunities to feel better about yourself than you ever have before. Seriously. What if you could discover the gems within the challenges? What if you could find a way to use it to support you in becoming more empowered?

In a different color pen, follow up your challenge statements with at least one way it helps you. For example:

- <u>I am too sensitive</u>: I am afraid I can't handle certain situations. I find that I am actually keeping myself from doing the things I want to do because of it.

My sensitive nature provides me with the ability to get a clear sense of the people I interact with, despite what they are saying. I can always sense it when something feels off to me in these moments. This saves me time, energy, and upset. My sensitive nature also helps me to serve others in a way that is heart-centered and intuitive. They really trust me because they can tell that I understand what they are experiencing. This provides me with a great asset as I coach and counsel other people.

- <u>I hate my body.</u> I wake up every morning in despair over the way I look when I see myself in the mirror. I am too embarrassed to wear shorts or a cute little dress. Sometimes I just want to crawl out of my skin!

Because of the challenge I have felt with my body over the years, I have made it a practice to meditate and pray regularly. Even though it started out as a way to alleviate suffering, it has turned into the greatest gift I have ever been given. I now experience, through prayer and meditation, more peace and love within my own self than I ever would have if I did not have to go to the depths of who and what I really am in order to take care of myself.

Keep this journal, and when you are feeling down or overwhelmed by your story, bring forward the benefits you are receiving as well. Brainstorm ways you can use it to serve others, connect to Spirit, and find empowerment. Everything in life has a silver lining around it. There is always a gift in our experiences. Always.

Chapter 4
The Rules

*No problem can be solved from the same level
of consciousness that created it.*

~ Albert Einstein

Whether aware of it or not, all human beings have a set of rules that influence them. Society's rules of what is acceptable and valuable are easy to see, such as having a good job, being tall and thin, and projecting unrealistic amounts of confidence. As individuals we take cues from society, and then refine the rules into what we believe will make us the most desirable and valuable versions of ourselves. In reality, what we are doing is trying to create value based on a set of standards that we never even consciously chose for ourselves. And then we create rules for how we should be, and follow them with reckless abandon. I have become clear over the years that the rules I held for who I am "supposed" to be in life, are directly connected to the rules I created around food and exercise. You see, the core agreements I made with myself were showing up everywhere. One such agreement was that I had to keep everything together… I could not fall apart or be a "mess."

This was something I was committed to at all costs. Frequently I was not doing okay but because I could not allow myself to simply allow my truth deep down, I created methods to try to feel okay inside… food and exercise being my number one go to.

I created rules of how much and how far, and I did not listen to anything but that part of my head that created the rules. I was too afraid not to listen. The rules created a sense of safety for me in what felt like an unsafe world, both inside and outside.

My thoughts consumed me as I plotted and planned, in total fear that I would somehow become interrupted and not be able to follow through on my strenuous exercise plans. What torture! I remember running until there was no possible way that I could have moved one more inch, running with shin splints, running at 5 am before school, and running in below zero degree weather.

What is really powerful to recognize is that I preferred to do those painful things rather than experience the thoughts and feelings that resulted when I did not listen to my inner rule-creator. I thought if I just adhered to the self-imposed protocol, I would be able to avoid the self-loathing that would come if I disobeyed. My daily mantra was, "You just have to get through this, and then you can relax."

It did not take long for a depression to kick in. After all, once the day's quota had been met, I had tomorrow's quota to consider. I lived in a never-ending state of trying to free myself from the wrath of my own mind, which of course could not be done because I was stuck in a state of trying to alleviate myself from myself. I was trying to find peace inside, but I did not understand that peace could not be found at the level of consciousness that the problem existed. Participating in compulsions to find peace kept me operating at a lower level of consciousness, and so real peace could not be found.

When I went through my initial stages of recovery from bulimia, my mind's desire to create rules was still operating. The rules were simply different now; I believed I had to feel certain things, behave certain ways, and eat just so. I thought if I went off course from the new rules I would be a failure. I still felt trapped and like I had very little room to breathe.

Although I was not damaging my body in the same way, my spirit still hurt.

What I learned over time is that looking at how I am relating to my challenges is everything. If I want to be free, then I need to look at the grip and attachment I have on things because that very grip is the issue. The tight grip on trying to "fix" myself was making things worse. I could not hear my guidance that resided at a higher level of consciousness – the consciousness that holds the solution.

I learned that I had to move into a place where I could allow all of my experience to exist, so I could get really honest about what that grip was all about. This gave me some breathing room to get in there and really see what was going on so I could learn what I needed. I was hooked to my rules for a reason, and until I could go in and find out what needs were not being met inside of myself, I would continue to try and meet them through the rules I had created.

Another thing I learned is that I needed to let all of my thoughts and feelings have a voice. Rather than just trying to shut them up, I had to start inquiring and listening so I could better understand what I needed deep down. I stopped making it about what it appeared to be about (the food and exercise), so I could explore what it was *really* about.

Activity: Bringing in the Light

I have three words for you – "the battle zone." Now I have four words for you – "Get out of there!" It does us no good to battle back and forth inside. Why? Because it would be impossible to win of course! How could you win a battle between two opposing sides when you own both of them? To win, you must shift your awareness to a new level where you can see from a higher perspective. This way you can stop fighting. And let's be honest, the fight is what is the most painful.

This is a foundational teaching that all great teachers speak of. From a spiritual perspective, as a whole, humanity is in a process of needing to go to a higher state of consciousness in order to relieve suffering. And for the healing battle between aspects of ourselves, we apply the same principle; we go higher than the opposing aspects. If we do not, we stay in the war. This is what AA is referring to when they say that the solution cannot be found at the same level of conscious it was created.

We do this by learning how to allow our small self (personality) to have her truth, while maintaining a connection to the absolute Truth. The absolute Truth is God, our Essence, our soul. It is the Light that transforms darkness, much like turning on a light switch in a dark room. Until that switch is flipped, we are often disoriented, not sure which way we should go. We must honor both our small self and our Essence. Our small self needs us to listen to it, acknowledge it, and help it. We can do this most powerfully by aligning ourselves with the knowing that our Essence, our soul, knows the way out. In service to creating a shift inside of you, from being totally identified with the small self, to being able to *help* the small self, complete the following activity:

Grab a pen and paper and find a quiet place where you will be uninterrupted. Relax your body and open up to the possibility that somewhere inside of you there is a space that can shine light on any situation. There is nothing too big. And with this hope, complete the following process:

1. Ask this inner place of Light how you can start to embrace your situation and write down what you hear.
2. Ask the Light what the message is for you to learn during this challenge. Write down what you hear.
3. Ask the Light what positive affirmation you are to start repeating to yourself to assist you in remembering this part of you. Write this down.
   Example: My Truth is I am a soul having a human experience.

Chapter 5
From Powerless to Finding Strength in the Divine Mother

The light of Guru's grace helps us to see and remove the obstacles in our path.

~ Amma

It goes without saying that I was desperate during the years of rules galore. I was searching for a sense of relief from my own self, including my fear and my judgments. I wanted to find peace and feel protected in the world. At the time I was only able to see the surface level of what was going on, yet there was obviously something very important inside needing my attention. I felt completely and utterly vulnerable. So I did what anyone would do; I came up with a way to experience a sense of protection and safety. This illusionary sense of safety was better than the terror I felt deep down. To me, the safety produced a real effect. It soothed me.

At the time I did not understand that my intense fears were being played out in my body image. I was acting out my deep fears about what comes with being human. The truth is we have no control, but instead we try to come up with ways in which we can experience the illusion of control. And naturally, we then come up with ways to comfort ourselves.

Part of life is pain and uncertainty, yet we do our best to create a different reality. As we try to lay a sturdy foundation to stand on, through cutting calories or jogging further, we lose connection to the one thing that actually brings about a true sense of security. We stop connecting to our real safety net: Spirit.

I can distinctly remember believing that if I could obtain the "perfect" body, things would not be so painful in life. I truly believed that if I looked a certain way, life's ups and downs would feel less chaotic or debilitating. I believed that hiding behind thin legs or less body fat would protect me from the vulnerability I felt.

This has all come into my awareness after the fact of course. At the time, I was not aware of my fear. Because I was so caught up in the rules, I was disconnected to the deeper fears and the feelings. It took a slow, steady dive into myself, and into my Self, to see the truth. It took many years to realize the compulsions themselves were not where I needed to focus my energy if I wanted freedom.

Although my conscious mind was not able to recognize how afraid I was, my dreams provided me with many clues. As a child I had repetitive dreams of Cookie Monster chasing me and not being able to run. I had many dreams that I was being abducted but could not move because I was frozen in terror. In these dreams, I was a victim to others and felt like I could not make it in the world. My dreams were showing me this night after night after night. But I did not understand. I was only a child.

Then on my eleventh birthday I experienced an event that shook me to my core. While vacationing with my family, two semi-trailer trucks were following our van on an old dirt road. We kept slowing down to scout for land where we could build a cabin. The constant stopping and going infuriated the truck drivers. They jumped out of their trucks and started beating the windows of our van, trying to break in. I thought they had a gun and did not know what would happen to us. I was terrified. My dad took off and they began chasing us down a winding gravel road. After an eternity of cat and mouse, we lost them and pulled into a nearby police station.

That night, when asked how I was doing, I told my family

that I was fine and not scared. I lied because, for some reason, I believed I had to keep it together. I am not sure why, but I believed I needed to keep my fearful state a secret. After a couple of months of trying to feel something different from what I was authentically experiencing, I started having panic attacks. By cutting off from something that needed to be worked through, it started to try and work itself out. My panic attacks were simply a symptom of something needing my attention. I was not paying attention to what I felt deep down, and the fear was now being expressed through a symptom, through panic attacks.

Our relationship with food operates in this exact same way. A conflicted relationship with food simply means there is something deep down that desperately needs our attention. That is it. It does not mean there is something wrong with us or that we are incapable of finding freedom. It just means we have not healed what needs our love yet.

At eleven years old, I was hyperventilating daily. I started to fear choking, and only ate certain foods that seemed least likely to get stuck in my throat. It did not take long before my diet consisted of applesauce, ice cream, and for some reason, one specific kind of cookie. I guess this just goes to show that unresolved fears do not necessarily play out in a way that makes logical sense. To this day I don't know why these specific foods were the ones I felt safe eating.

I would never have linked my fear of choking and my panic attacks to the unresolved trauma I experienced from the trucker incident. All I saw was that I was afraid of not being able to breathe and that I had to try at all costs to get through the day without passing out from a panic attack. The panic attacks, and even worse, my fear of them, seemed to be the problem. But the truth is they really weren't the issue. The issue was the feeling I held deep down of being powerless and a victim to life's uncertainties. That is what was generating the symptoms. Years later I can see what the driving force was underneath what was happening. Again, this holds true for challenges with food as well.

That is the slippery slope of trying to resolve food challenges: people spend so much energy dealing with what they are experiencing on the surface, that they don't really tune into what is driving the behavior at the core. When we can take the time to explore what the most basic and fundamental driving force is, we create the opportunity to address and heal it.

To support you in connecting with what is going on at the deepest level, start to explore what is underneath the symptoms.

Dive into what is beneath conscious awareness, letting go of trying to figure out why you do what you do. Allow yourself to have permission to think outside the box. You will not "figure it out," but it can be revealed to you. You want to go all the way into the places inside that are vulnerable and afraid. These are the places that keep you locked into your coping patterns, because they are desperate for help.

Tell me about this part of you that is so afraid. Take a look at her vulnerability. Tap into this energy. Let it be okay that you are an adult walking around with the tenderness of a sweet, innocent child that needs some help. We all have this place inside of us.

To do this, you are going to work with your inner child and inner parent. The magnitude of relief that can come from working with our inner child is astonishing. This is precisely why my Spiritual Psychology professors, Dr. Ron and Mary Hulnick, honed in on the healing aspects of this work. It teaches us how to stop suppressing, creates a way to be compassionate and loving with the places inside that hurt, and teaches us how to start supporting ourselves in the ways that we needed all along.

The power here comes in fully allowing your younger self to express her feelings, void of any judgment. This is essential.

Allow her to have the dignity to fully express herself without fear of being judged. She desperately needs to know she has a safe container in which to express herself. You are her safe container.

This container is created organically by bringing forward your most loving inner parent. I encourage you to consider your inner parent to be the Divine Mother, who is the embodiment of pure, unconditional love. It is this love that makes is safe to be vulnerable. It is this love that heals and protects. It is a loving response from the Divine Mother that helps us find the Light. In this Light we are always safe and sheltered from harm. She always holds people in complete safety in her loving arms.

Activity: The Divine Mother's Eyes

Create a time in your schedule where you will have plenty of privacy and a quiet environment. I invite you to pull out candles, incense, oils, and anything else that assists you in relaxing. Take at least five minutes and concentrate on your heart center. Just feel your heart and the love that beats within it. Relax.

Part 1: Opening to the Divine Mother

The mother is an archetype, an energy, a way of being that each one of us possesses. What can vary is how in tune with this energy a person is, and how willing one is to let the mother energy soothe the inner child. To begin, we consider the qualities of the mother energy. For me personally, I call upon the Divine Mother because it joins the two things I crave most when I am hurting; the supreme love and wisdom of the Divine, and the comfort and care of the mother.

The Divine Mother is unconditionally loving, infinitely compassionate, and full of nurturing energy. She is always available to you and wants to love you. The way you imagine her to look is completely up to you; just focus on the beautiful and loving entity that she is.

Complete the following in your journal:
1. What does the Divine Mother look like to you?
2. What qualities does your Divine Mother have?
   Examples: Unconditionally loving, compassionate, wise, safe, etc.
3. Ask Her if she will start to become a part of your everyday life and write down what this loving, Divine Mother would tell you in times of need.

Part 2: The Meeting

Now that you are anchored in the energy of the Divine Mother, take yourself on a journey back in time to when you were a little girl. Think back to a moment when you were going through a hard time. Through the eyes of the wise and all-loving mother energy, allow your younger self to share with you what she needed during that time. Was it acceptance, validation, or perhaps to simply know that she would be taken care of? Ask *her* what she needed during this difficult time. Write down what your younger self needed in your journal.

Part 3: Meeting Our Own Needs

Thinking back once again to the brilliance of the unconditionally loving Divine Mother energy, consider how this place within you can start to nourish your younger self. Whatever she brought forward as her need, your job becomes to meet it as best you can. To support you in this, complete the following:

1. As the mother of my younger self, my intention is to help her by _____.
   Example: Being a loving parent to her.

2. Because I know she needs _____, I will do this by _____.

   Example: love, telling her she matters.

Chapter 6
Healing through Creative Expression

The body heals with play, the mind heals with laughter, and the spirit heals with joy.

~ Proverb

As I peeled back the layers of what was at the core of my food and exercise addiction, I began to recall childhood memories that mirrored what was happening in my life as an adult. I remember this intense desire to play, freely express myself, and exchange positive energy with those around me. When it was not available I ached for it. I felt lonely, sad, and would numb out with television and food. This same pattern was happening in my life as an adult. Recognizing this was helpful in that it illuminated the depression I was experiencing, but just seeing the pattern was not enough. I had to get to the core of what I was really yearning for and find a way to give myself what I needed. An understanding was not going to satiate this deep hunger I felt. I needed to learn how to fulfill the part of me that never felt fulfilled as a child.

As a kid, I remember waking up every day with so much love in my heart I felt as though I was going to burst. The amount of sheer joy I felt was uncontainable. As soon as my eyes opened I would be overcome with gratitude for life itself. I would leap out of bed and run out to my family as though it was Christmas morning. I couldn't contain the love in me and had to share it. My little heart was bursting at the seams. This love, this Divine love, is something that naturally expresses itself and is a creative force that cannot be contained.

Because part of being human is living with limitations, our parents absolutely cannot meet every single need we have as children. The same law will hold true for those of us who become parents ourselves. We simply cannot meet another's every need and desire. We are not meant to. This is God's job. It is an inside job.

But as a child, these unmet needs impact us. We take it personally and we start to adjust our natural expression so we blend in with our surroundings, which usually involves our dimming our light in some way. When the love I was pouring out was not reciprocated in the way I needed it to be, I was devastated. I remember being disappointed, yet adorably, if I say so myself, continuing to try day after day to play in this heart space with others. Eventually I gave up because it hurt too much when I was not met. And because I did not know any better, I felt as though my light was not important, that I was not important. And so I started to disconnect from the natural expression that was within me.

When I stopped my natural state of creative expression, I stopped connecting to my heart. This left me feeling unfulfilled and aching for the intimacy that could only be found when I was attuned to the creative energy within me. As I journeyed through my recovery process, and opened back up to this creative energy, I got to taste the sweetness of this long lost part of me. Oh how I had missed feeling playful and free to just express myself! I realized I needed this in my life in order to feel fulfilled and happy. I needed to get out of my head and let my child-like heart simply share itself.

Because I had shut this place down within me, it felt awkward at first trying to tune back in and share myself with the world. I found myself believing that I needed others to draw my playful side out of me. Then I realized I would have to spend the rest of my life waiting on others to help me be happy and free if I did not learn how to express myself on my own. I stopped handing my permission-to-play card to others and started to rise up on my own behalf. I stopped the happiness excuse train. If what I wanted was to experience the sheer joy of my free, inner-childlike nature, then I had to consider what activities help me attune to that energy within me.

    Recently a friend came to visit me. We drove up to a near-by regional park and began hiking into the woods. Not being able to contain myself a moment longer, following that straight and narrow path, I let go of inhibiting my creative self. The next thing I knew we spent an hour climbing trees and pretending we were the king and queen of the forest as we shouted to our kingdom, sharing our prophecies and good fortune. We ran around, doing things that children enjoy, sprinting back and forth for no good reason at all. My friend is very tall, so whenever he was standing with his legs apart I could not seem to help myself from running and diving through his legs!

    This time in the woods together was exactly what I needed. I did not need to have a conversation about why I was feeling bored that morning, or how I used to feel as a child. No deep inner work is needed at all. Sometimes all we need is to stop being so serious and let ourselves be open and express our creative intelligence! I was clear that all I needed that day was to participate in life in the way my soul was aching for. I needed to have the experience of this creative energy running through my body. I just needed my adult self to take a back seat for a while and stop trying to think my way into joy, so I could be with my playful self.

I have learned that my relationship to food is influenced by the level of creative expression I have in my life at a given time. I am more drawn to want to eat compulsively when I am not experiencing the joy that comes from allowing my inner child to play freely. I have learned that compulsive eating and cravings are not my issue. My issue is that during these times, I am not giving myself what I need, which generates cravings and a strong pull toward food when I am not really hungry. *By allowing the child-like joy and playfulness to be expressed and experienced, I feed the real craving.*

Activity: Child-like Play, Creative Freedom and Expression

This activity requires that you connect with your inner child and allow yourself to have fun! Your inner child does not care about all the serious stuff, and she certainly does not care what she looks like as she plays in the world. This is a time to let your guard down and say good-bye to any filters you may have. The sole purpose is to open up and be free! All you need to do is connect to your inner child, the place within you that is carefree and likes to express herself however she feels in the moment.

Simply think back to the activities that brought you the most joy as a child. Was it swimming in pool? Riding your bike? Dancing? Whatever your child liked to do then is a great place to start.

Tuning into your inner child, ask *her* the following:

1. What do you feel like doing?
2. What sounds fun to you?
3. Write down her responses.
4. Keep this list and refer to it when you start to notice old habitual patterns of depression, anxiety or loneliness.

Then simply commit yourself to the activity at least one time in the upcoming week. Try out what she says sounds like fun. What do you have to lose?

Let loose and be in the flow!

Chapter 7
Setting an Intention

The flowers of all the tomorrows are planted in the seeds of today.
~ Ancient Chinese Proverb

I started eighth grade in September of 1994 as a normal and healthy teenager. Within several months I was fighting for my life in the hospital. Whatever happened that made that downward spiral happen so quickly still eludes me. I honestly have no idea. I was dropping weight so quickly that my body was shutting down, which explains a few things, such as my inability to recognize that I needed help.

Although my in-patient treatment for anorexia was not voluntary, I am grateful because it saved my life. After I left my hospital stay, I learned just how important it is to be in a solid place on all levels before moving on; my body was restored to a healthy weight, but my mind and emotions still needed a lot of tending. The restoration and healing of the mind is a process that takes place over a period of time. Unfortunately, all too often, people backslide because they were not ready to leave. This was certainly my experience.

The day I was discharged I was thrilled to go home. I experienced several months of following my treatment protocol, and I tried the best I could to maintain my weight. However, in time, my weight plummeted back down. When I tried to get it back up, I could not handle the guilt I was feeling as I tried to force massive amounts of food into my body. I was trying to meet the weight I had to be at in order to appease the doctors. But, the guilt was too much so I began purging.

Shortly after, I had a vision of all the bulimics that were in the hospital with me. I remembered hearing how common it was to move from anorexia to bulimia.

And then I heard the only sane thing I had heard from my head in months, "You cannot do this, Lesley ... not alone. You are not capable of doing this on your own." In that moment, I knew this to be true in my bones. It was a moment that something larger, something outside of my human mind, came in and guided me. And I thankfully listened. I had my first experience of complete surrender and humility. I told my family I needed help again, and that this time I really wanted it.

When we arrived back at the eating disorder treatment unit the second time, they asked me, "Why should we let you back in?" Confused by the callousness of the staff, I just cried. I didn't know what to say. I certainly could understand why they wouldn't want to bring back the girl who showed other patients how to hide their food during meal-time. I was told, "If *you* don't want to get better, Lesley, it doesn't do you any good to come back here." I assured him this time I was serious. And I was. I had heard my guidance and thank God I was able to honor it.

This time, during meals, my butter was the first thing in my mouth, as opposed to trying to slap it on the underside of the dining room table when no one was looking. And the nurses noticed this shift in me. In fact they sat in disbelief as I ate my food with such determination. The second hospitalization was still challenging and a lot of hard work, but I stuck to my intention to get better.

The intention to re-connect with my heart and soul while moving through the physical healing kept me focused on what I wanted most in my life. It became something I was holding for, no matter what my thoughts and feelings were in any given moment. I wanted freedom!

Activity: Creating an Intention

An important step in creating the life you desire is setting an intention that hones in on what you really want for yourself. The purpose of this is to assist you in shifting your focus from what you do not want, to what you do want.

The first time I experienced the power of this was when I was studying with Dr. Ron and Mary Hulnick. They were very clear about the power of intention. They drew a substantial amount of their information from the work of Wayne Dyer. What I have learned over the years is how easy it can be to focus on what we don't want, what we want to stop, and what we want to get rid of.

This is not helpful because it means that we are facing the wrong direction. We must turn around and start to focus on what it is that we do want to create in our lives. You see, it is from here that the path can be determined.

This provides you with the opportunity to continue to grow into what you want to experience in life. You get to take steps into what you want to cultivate, rather than drowning in what is not working.

For example, "It is my intention to cultivate a positive and healthy relationship to food, exercise, and my body." Notice that I did not write, "My intention is to stop being so demanding on myself." Notice how you feel after you read each sentence. The first intention creates an opening inside of us, whereas the second intention leaves an energy of deflation. Because energy follows what we think about, we want to hone in on what we do want. In other words, if you are feeling challenged with food, asking yourself how not to struggle is not fruitful. Instead, in this example, ask yourself what choices you would need to have a healthy relationship with food.

And don't be afraid to be really honest with yourself. This process isn't about focusing about getting rigid with your life. It is about gaining heartfelt clarity and then becoming willing to get whatever level of support you need.

Complete the following process:
Grab a pen and paper and find a peaceful setting where you will not be interrupted by others. If you meditate, setting your

intention after your practice is a great way to create from a place of clarity and calm. After you are centered, inquire within what it is that your heart wants for you. Ask what it is you want to be experiencing in life more than anything. Begin to write down what comes forward without censoring. After you feel complete, go over the list and focus in on what seems to be the most important thing for you *at this time* in your life.

Once you have your intention on paper, put it somewhere you will see it every day. Put it in your bedroom, bathroom or car. Support yourself in your process by reading it out loud daily. Do whatever it is that would support you in creating this intention in your life.

Chapter 8
Hope

Dear One, if you get tired of trying to do everything on your own, just let me know and I will help you. Love, God.

~ Doreen Virtue

My desire to recover during my second hospitalization carried me for a while, and it was lovely. I channeled all my energy into my healing process. I gave all I could. After a few weeks of trying to find strength from my own will power, I hit my limit of what I was capable of doing on my own. I needed help. I needed courage, strength, and love to carry me through. In exhaustion, I collapsed into the fetal position on the cold hospital floor. I wailed and cried from the very depths of my being. In between tears, I humbly asked God to help me through this. *I resigned from my position as the leader of my recovery.*

And then a miracle happened. I felt the presence of something angelic, something Divine. And although I did not hear the words through my ears, I received the message, "You can do this. I will help you. You are not alone." I felt warm and safe. And just like that, hope was breathed back into me. Just like I had cried from the depths of my being, I was *filled* to the depths of my being, but this time, with hope.

Hope is necessary in life. Without it, the potential for a brighter future cannot exist. So what do you do when you have little to no hope? You call upon God and ask for a miracle, that is what you do! You ask that something more powerful than you have ever known shows you the truth of what is possible. At this point, your task is to continuously remain open; humble yourself and allow God to talk to you. This is done by not trying to find the answer in your own head. Let that approach go. If it has not worked so far, why would it work now? Surrender your own way to that of something higher. Open yourself up to the wildest of miracles. *Drop into your heart and ask to be met.*

Activity: Heart-Centered Prayer

When we pray, we can express ourselves from our head or our heart. When we pray from our heart, we come into a deeper resonance with ourselves and allow the prayer to be led from the depths of our soul. There is no right way to pray, yet I do believe that when it comes from your heart and soul, magic happens. Why? Because you are coming from a different place, the place that connects you to the Beloved. How can you hear God speaking to your heart if you are stuck in your head?

Whatever the prayer is when we pray from our hearts, we *feel* the prayer. Use your senses to your advantage. Let these sensations be in your body and guide your process through this sacred time.

Decide on a time where you will have five minutes to yourself every day. Just upon waking or just prior to sleep is ideal.

1. Place your hand on your heart and connect to this place of love and wisdom inside of you. Your connection comes simply by bringing your awareness to your heart and being with it. Allow your awareness to shift from the head down into your body. Give yourself permission to slow down and be with this powerful heart that sustains you.

2. After a couple minutes being with this connection, *feel* your prayer to Spirit. Let your heart ask for what it yearns for. Your heart wants high vibrational things, such as peace, love, joy, and freedom. Your head is the part of you that is attached to how you think this will come about. *When we pray from our head we ask for things to be a certain way. When we pray from our heart we ask God to show us the way.*

Let your heart lead your prayer. Release attachment to the outcome. Allow the Grace of the Universe. Prayer is a powerful tool that, when uttered from our heart, has the power to move mountains. Our only job when we pray is to get out of the way, to release what we think will be the solution and our salvation, and completely surrender to a consciousness that is higher than our pain and suffering. This is the genius of it all. We don't have to know the way, and this means we can finally stop wasting our precious energy trying to figure it all out.

Let God breathe wisdom into your beating heart. All you need to do is stay present to this place inside of you. Your heart has the answer. Are you willing to listen to it?

Chapter 9
Creating Your Destiny

What is now proved was once only imagined.
~ William Blake

After my powerful experience on the hospital floor, I was more determined than ever to move beyond my inner limitations. I wanted a life in which I gave myself more than just the crumbs. With a steadfast approach to my recovery, I started ninth grade with a healthy body. Although my physical wellbeing was not an issue at this time, I still was not free from my mind's incessant need to monitor my every move, judge, and try to control things. In other words, I still felt completely trapped by my mind.

Although there was great improvement in my life, I still had a lot of inner pain and fear to work with. Because I did not know how to effectively handle it, this is the time I began an eleven-year journey with bulimia. Bulimia allowed me to completely avoid feelings and thoughts that were painful to sit with. Bulimia was an escape portal when I felt like there was no way out of my inner reality. But in time I learned that it was not a helpful escape route, as it never really got me to where I wanted to go. I simply moved from one jail cell to another.

I did my best to find happiness during this time. I pushed aside the truth of my situation. Rather than stepping into and dealing with how trapped I felt, I just tried to keep my life going. I tried to date, furthered my education, and took a new job every so often. But the truth was, no matter what I was doing in the external world, my internal world was one in which I felt stagnant and unfulfilled.

And then the day came eleven years later when I decided I wanted out of the cell I was dwelling in. I dreamed of a life where I was free to move and be as I pleased. I wanted to travel with friends, be able to live with my partner, and create the space to fulfill my soul's destiny on this planet. It was the dream within my heart that called me forward into a dedicated "yes" to this next phase of my recovery process. Never once in those eleven years did the pain get bad enough for me to make this declaration. It was my soul that pulled me through. I kept seeing myself looking back on my life in my old age, consumed with grief for never being able to live a life that reflected what was in my heart and soul, the love I wanted to offer and share with the world. This deeper desire is what ultimately led me to take the next step.

Soul's Wisdom

Deep within me there was nothing I wanted more than to love others when they were suffering. As a kid I saw myself living in Africa, amongst the tribes of starving children, feeding them, loving them, and consoling them. And although at twenty-seven I did not necessarily think I would be moving to Africa, I wanted to live a life of altruism. I wanted to give back to others and the world, and not be caught up in my own "stuff." In other words, I wanted to fulfill my soul's calling. I wanted what Africa represented to me. *And this day, the day my soul became louder than my mind, was the day my life changed forever.*

It is here, in our soul's deep wisdom, that our solutions arise. I have never *thought* my way out of any challenge. Solutions always come from this deeper place within me. They come from the love of my heart and the guidance of my spirit.

The mind can be sneaky when we start to listen to our heart and soul's calling. It may not believe this deeper wisdom can be trusted. It even may choose to rebel against it. That is where the work comes in. That is where choice comes in. And that is where Grace comes in. It is always up to us in any given moment to choose what we are listening to. Choice is one of the most powerful forces on Earth, because from it, we have the opportunity to create what we want. And as our first step, we can start by listening to what our soul has to say.

Activity: What Does Your Soul Have to Say?

As the keeper of your life force, your soul is here to support you. It is here to bring you to a place of freedom, joy, and fulfillment. It wants you to fulfill your destiny and to wake up to your greatness. You are here to wake up to your own Divinity and fulfill your soul's contract for your life.

Part 1: Soul Inquiry

Grab a pen and your journal. Find a quiet place where you will be uninterrupted. Play a piece of music that really opens your heart up, something that speaks to you on a very deep level. Then answer the following questions:

1. What is the deepest place inside of me yearning for?
2. Who do I want to be in the world?
3. What would be a dream come true for this life?

Part 2: Your Soul's Wisdom Collage

Buy a poster board, glue, markers, and other fun materials. Create a vision board, a Soul's Wisdom board, for what you discovered today. Cut out any photos, write any words, decorate, create, and get excited about what your soul shares with you. This is your opportunity to create your future on a blank canvas.

Chapter 10
Honesty and the Beauty of Vulnerability

You have been criticizing yourself for years and it hasn't worked. Try approving of yourself and see what happens.

~ Louise Hay

In due time, I came to realize that the 12 steps were not providing me with what I personally was looking for. Although I believe they are incredibly valuable and I have great respect for them, certain aspects of the program simply stopped resonating for me. I chose to continue my journey back to my Self in other ways. Coming back to the Self is a life-long journey, and I learned that what supports me at one time is not necessarily what will always support me.

What was true for us in the past may not be true for us in the present.

That being said, there have been some constants that have gone unchanged in my life. No matter what person I was talking to, which group I was attending, or what training I was learning, there were key ingredients that I always needed in order to get the most out of my experience. These key ingredients were, and still are, honesty and vulnerability.

Honesty and vulnerability can never become an unnecessary part of our journey because they are a path out of the places we don't want to face. And as long as we are suffering, there is something we do not want be with, something we don't want to be true. And thread within what we don't want to face is often a sense of shame. But thankfully for us, there is an antidote to shame. This antidote is vulnerability. Vulnerability is the medicine. It is a doorway out, and it paves the way to freedom from the confines of our judgments.

It is in the ownership of our real feelings about ourselves and our lives that open the door to allow the rejected parts of ourselves be seen and loved. My mentor and friend, John Welshons, describes this as bringing our darkness to the Light. In other words, we take what we are rejecting about ourselves and bring it to a loving place. Just as Dr. King said, "Hate cannot drive out hate: only love can do that."

Our perceived darkness is not really darkness in a negatives sense of the word. It is simply the parts that we have hidden away into the dark nooks and crannies within us, so we don't have to look at them. Once we learn that we are loveable no matter what we have said, think, do and feel, we no longer need to hide things away. Imagine this. Imagine all of a sudden all the places inside that had dark, looming clouds over them, were all of a sudden blasted with radiant sunshine. It is a total game changer. It is as though we get to emerge from a long, dark winter, into a warm summer day.

Imagine how freeing you would feel if the heaviness associated with shame were completely lifted. Imagine how free you would feel if you no longer had to try and compensate for the parts of yourself that you feel need to be fixed? You could just be! The amount of energy you would have available to you would increase exponentially!

Let's begin moving into the Light by being more honest with ourselves. Being radically honest with ourselves is what is most important. Who you share with beyond yourself and God is up to you. You get to decide what is in your best interest. For now, I invite you to do the following activity:

Activity: Getting Truthful

Answer the following questions:
1. What areas of my life am I carrying shame around?
2. Why do I believe I need to hide?
3. What does my mind tell me could happen if I am honest?
4. How can I take my first step toward being honest with myself from here on out?
5. Is there anything I am too afraid to face? Am I willing to hand this over to God?
6. What fears of self-perceptions do I need God to help me carry?

Now, complete the following:

Go to the mirror and look yourself in the eyes. Look deep. Go beyond the eyes themselves, using them as the gateway to the soul.

Simply say, "I love you," as you gaze into your eyes. Repeat again and again until you experience a shift into more love and compassion.

Chapter 11
Your Soul's Compass

Listen and attend with the ear of your heart.
~ Saint Benedict

Although completing my Master's in Spiritual Psychology was something I felt very positive about, it paled in comparison to awakening to the knowing that I am an infinitely worthy Being. Achieving an external goal is exciting and satisfying, yet the heart and soul want so much more. There is an inner goal that is embedded within us all, and that is to continue our awaking process so that we are in union with God. In this place, the personality self does not impact us, we do not suffer, and we know the Truth. It is here that we are truly free. For me, this has always been one of my deepest desires, although I will be the first to admit, my personality can sure get in the way!

I understand intellectually that I am infinitely worthy, but I am human. Therefore, embodying this Truth is a lifelong journey. Sometimes it feels easy and sometimes it doesn't. What always remains true, is that spending time connecting to the love inside of me is what makes all the difference.

Our soul is designed to continue to awaken. That is why we are here. Our time on Earth is in service to our soul's evolution. We come to learn lessons and to continue to awaken to the Love that is all-true and all-knowing. We are here to uncover who we really are. And, because we have lots to learn, we go through many situations (and lifetimes) that are designed to help us to continue to awaken. Food challenges, and all that goes with them, show us where we have pain and fear, so we can heal it and come back into resonance with our inherent truth.

Our challenges serve our soul's evolution. They are designed to help us wake up. We get to decide whether we hold our challenges as the enemy or as the teacher. We can fight them or we can use them as the gateway to our empowered and liberated self.

If we do not acknowledge where we are feeling challenged, we have to keep running away, stuffing, and disconnecting. For me, I know each day I have a choice. And that choice is whether or not I will run away or use the challenges to grow into who I want to be. *I have the power to stand for my soul's evolution and growth rather than pacify my ego.* We all do.

I do this through the little choices I make each day. I do it through being real, authentic, and getting messy. I let myself fall apart if I need to. I try to go in instead of looking out. I dive deep in search of the love within me, instead of finding someone to show me my worth. I let myself make mistakes and I course-correct as I go along. I give my all to my growth, totally and imperfectly. I fall. I get up. I forget. I remember.

I live a wildly human life, and I honor my soul for keeping me on the track back home to Truth. This life is what I make of it, with or without an eating disorder. I am my own liberator, just as you are yours. The answers are within you, because you are the Divine in flesh. This is my promise to you.

Activity: You As Guru

This activity is designed to lead you to the place within that is your North Star, your guiding light. To get the most out of this experience, I encourage you to prepare for it by spending a significant amount of time quieting yourself and slowing down. The more peaceful you are, the easier it is to hear your guidance. Spend a few hours engaging in whatever activity will connect you to your Essence. You may hike, sit by the ocean, or spend an afternoon in silence. Whatever it is, partake in it fully. This is *for* you. This is not something you have to do. This is something you *get* to do. Time with you is sacred. It is a gift you get to give yourself. Cherish it.

After you have completed the activity of your choosing, ask yourself the following questions:

1. What miracle do I need from Spirit for me to be happy, joyous, and free in this life?

2. If there were no excuses (money, time, lack of professional help, etc.), what do I need in place in order to have this experience?

3. Trusting that my inner guidance is here to serve me and that it is on my side, what small step can I take today that will support me in moving toward my miracle life? What is one small way I can commit to this dream I have for myself?

Chapter 12
Celebration

I celebrate myself, and sing myself.
~ Walt Whitman

Have you bowed down to your greatness today? You, my dear sister, have many things to acknowledge yourself for. How do I know? I know because it is far too common to bypass celebrating ourselves. Focusing on what we don't like, rather than what we do, is the norm unfortunately. It is time for this to change. No more fixing. No more "I am not enough." No more ignoring our greatness.

The time has come to create a new way of living. It is your time. And you are worthy of your own love. Think about the way we acknowledge those in our life that we are close to. We write them cards, throw parties, and tell them why we think they are so amazing. We see the ways they are awesome, and now it's time to send some of this love to ourselves.

I seem to have been born a natural cheerleader. I see so much beauty in others and I share openly how I view them. I honor them. I invite them to start honoring themselves. This one act, self-honoring, lights people up. It is such a beautiful thing to see someone own who they are. It is not conceited. It is just plain inspiring!

And just like we can step into celebrating our greatness on the inside, we can also celebrate greatness on the outside. If you have made it this far in this process, you have much to acknowledge yourself for. Just look at all the ways you have shown up for yourself. You, my dear, are here, still reading, still going, still engaged. And that, in and of itself, is worthy of acknowledgment and celebration. I honor you.

By focusing on what you have done and what you continue to do, you create the opportunity for good feelings to arise. This is a truly amazing gift you can give yourself anytime, anywhere. Stop and acknowledge yourself. Be proud. You are in charge of celebrating you. Be that person. Throw yourself a party. Why not? It is only weird if you think it is.

I have had my own personal experience with bypassing the positive and focusing on the negative. And today I say

"No more!" I stand for who I am, and the journey I have walked. I acknowledge myself for never giving up and for continuing to grow and evolve into a heart-centered woman. I honor myself for my dedication to Spirit. I am proud of myself for listening to my inner voice, being willing to move outside of my comfort zone, and stepping into my purpose work. There is much to celebrate.

Recognizing on the mental level where we can honor ourselves is important, yet it is only a part of the process. Celebrating is something we do, something we participate in. We have to show up to our own party, as both the giver and the receiver. As the giver we create the time and space to honor ourselves.

We connect to our hearts and listen to what we want to honor in ourselves. We share openly all the greatness we see. As the recipient we take an open stance, allowing the words to touch our hearts. We savor them and let them dance through our bodies.

By regularly allowing ourselves to throw a little party in our own honor, we are jump-starting our own well-being. We are becoming more responsible for our own happiness. And most importantly, we are giving to ourselves what we most deserve, our own love and adoration.

Activity: Your Celebration Ritual

This is your party, so naturally, it is all about you! I encourage you to celebrate yourself as a way of life, pausing and acknowledging at least one way you are showing up for yourself on a regular basis. And to get the ball rolling, we are going to start by participating in a more formal affair. A party for you. This activity requires that you have some fun! It requires that you think up at least one thing you can celebrate yourself for, and that you actually participate in a celebration ritual. Again, this is for fun! This is for you! So enjoy yourself!

Pull out a piece of paper and a pen. I invite you to participate fully in the following:

- Create a list of at least five things that you acknowledge yourself for.
- Choose one from your list that has the most heart for you.
- Create a fun and simple way you can celebrate and honor yourself for the one you choose off your list.
- Pick a day to spend time celebrating yourself.
- Make it enjoyable.

Examples of ways to celebrate yourself:

- Create an afternoon just for you. Take the time to acknowledge yourself and then celebrate by doing something you love.

- Treat yourself to a solo date night.

- Host a dinner party where each guest comes ready to honor and celebrate themselves.

- Look in the mirror and tell yourself all the ways you have grown since participating in these activities.

Continuing the Journey

Thank you for joining me and letting me share my journey with you. You honor me by taking my words to heart and using the activities in the book to enhance your own life.

There is so much more to share and explore in our beautiful and expanded lives! We can continue our journey together if you'd like to visit my website, **LesleyWirth.com**, and join my mailing list. It will be my pleasure to keep you informed about opportunities to go deeper in the work we have done so far.

Opportunities include:

- One-on-one, very personalized coaching.

- Participation in a 12-week program with a group.

- Participation in the 12-week program on your own so as to get more attention.

You will also have the opportunity to participate in a weekend immersion at a gorgeous location. This will be a small group activity where we will hone in on the inner child and Divine Mother work. This will be a once-in-a-lifetime gift that each participant will give to the others in the group. *Inspired* is the best word to describe the weekend.

Please let others know about the book and direct them to **LesleyWirth.com** for more information. This work is sacred, touching the lives of women all over the world who need to receive a message of hope and comfort around food and body image. Thank you for helping me let others receive.

Love and Light,

Lesley

About the Author

LESLEY WIRTH is a transformational coach, spiritual counselor, and author of *Own Your Worth: A Spiritual Journey through Food Compulsion to Self-Love.* Her formal education and experience transcending anorexia, bulimia, compulsive exercising, and overeating led her to teach how "food freedom" unleashes a more beautiful life.

Lesley is dedicated to supporting women who are ready to get to the core of what keeps them bound to food behaviors that no longer serve their highest and best selves. She is a sought after coach with a recipe for vanquishing pain and shame that worked miraculously in her own personal transformation.

With a Master's in Spiritual Psychology and years of study under naturopathic doctors and healers, Lesley identified the deep, unmet needs among women who wish to truly succeed in their relationship to food. She then developed a three-month program designed to teach women how to take dominion over their inner state and use their soul's wisdom to rise above old patterns.

Today Lesley works closely with clients creating fulfilling lives that reflect their newfound freedom with food. Her work is being implemented in spiritual communities, yoga studios, and recovery centers.

Notes

Notes

Notes

Notes

Notes

Notes

www.ingramcontent.com/pod-product-compliance
Lightning Source LLC
Chambersburg PA
CBHW072159100426
42738CB00011BA/2475